THE

Demaundes Joyous

A FACSIMILE OF THE FIRST ENGLISH RIDDLE BOOK, EDITED WITH AN INTRODUCTION AND NOTES BY JOHN WARDROPER

GORDON FRASER LONDON 1976

This edition first published 1971 by The Gordon Fraser Gallery Ltd., London and Bedford
Reprinted 1976

ISBN 0 900406 19 4 paperback

The facsimile of the 1511 edition of *The Demaundes Joyous*
has been made with the permission of the Syndics of the Cambridge University Library

Set in Monotype Ehrhardt and printed in Great Britain by T. H. Brickell & Son Ltd., The Blackmore Press, Gillingham, Dorset.

CONTENTS

INTRODUCTION

The little book presented here is doubly precious. It is the first collection of riddles printed in England; and only one copy is known to survive. Entertaining books from the early days of printing are particularly rare, for they tended to be read to tatters. Another example from the reign of Henry VIII is *A Hundred Merry Tales* which went on being printed into Shakespeare's time at least, and yet we have only one complete copy, from 1525 — because someone took it to Germany, where it lay unread until the eighteenth century. What chance it was that saved *The Demaundes Joyous* we cannot know. By the late seventeenth century it had found its way into a collection of early English books made by a Bishop of Ely, John Moore. After his death in 1714, his library was bought and given to Cambridge University by George I, and there the *Demaundes* have stayed.

Riddling, like jokemaking, has always been an art rich in bawdry. What varies from age to age and from country to country is the freedom with which the bawdry is written down. Some of the *Demaundes* are certainly coarse; but it is interesting to discover that the compiler (in the third year of Henry VIII's reign, not a time of delicate manners) was in fact a somewhat prudish man. His main source was a French collection, *Demandes joyeuses en maniere de quolibets,* of which the British Museum has one of the few surviving copies. A comparison shows that in borrowing twenty-nine of the eighty-seven French *demandes,* Wynkyn de Worde's compiler rejected a great number of obscene and scatological ones. Of those he did choose, he toned several down. Now, this act of censorship in 1511 would not be enough on its own to support a general theory of wholesome English restraint in the face of French outrageousness. However, there is a good deal of other evidence that over a long period the French were more daring, at least in writing. The ribaldry of their medieval fabliaux, for example, or of their Renaissance tales and songs, is much more wanton and copious. A glance, then, at the untranslated riddles in *Demandes joyeuses* can provide a pleasant footnote to literary history. To quote all the items whose answers contain the word *con* might be offensive, and would certainly take a great deal of space, so here are only three:

> ***Qui sont les deux meilleures choses en un ménage, et plus nécessaires?***
> ***—C'est le vit et le con; car sans le vit et le con on ne ferait jamais les noces.***
>
> (What are the two best and most necessary things in a household? — The prick and the cunt; for without the prick and the cunt you would never have any marriages.)
>
> ***Qu'est-ce que plus on quiert et moins on le trouve?***
> ***—C'est le fond d'un con.***
>
> (What is that which the more one seeks it, the further one is from it?—That is the bottom of a cunt.)
>
> ***Qui est le plus subtil bucher qui soit?***
> ***—C'est un con; car il tire la moelle des os sans les casser.***
>
> (What is the most artful butcher there is?
> —That is a cunt; for it extracts the marrow from bones

without breaking them.)

Farting was a source of merriment acceptable to the English compiler; but he did not take all that the French book had to offer. For example, he refused this:

> ***Comment partiriez-vous une vesse en deux?***
> ***—Mettez votre nez dedans mon cul. Vos deux narines le partiront justement, car autant en prendra l'une comme l'autre.***
> (How would you divide one fizzle in two?
> —Put your nose in my arse. Your two nostrils will divide it exactly, for one of them will take as much of it as the other.)

When people had been familiar for more than a century with Chaucer's way of dividing a fart into twelve (in the Summoner's Tale), it is a little surprising to see this barred. The ***Demandes joyeuses*** include some more solid pieces of anal humour which perhaps were rightly excluded. Such as:

> ***Comment feriez-vous de deux vieilles choses une neuve?***
> ***—Mangez deux vieux étrons. Vous en chierez un tout neuf.***
> (How would you make one new thing from two old ones?— Eat two old turds. You will shit one entirely new one.)

Another anal ***demande,*** a milder one, turns up in English much later, in a lawyer's manuscript collection of about 1620, and then in ***Wit Revived,*** a miscellany printed in 1655:

> ***Comment estouperiez-vous trois trous d'une cheville?***
> ***—Mettez votre nez en mon cul et vous estouperez mon cul de vos deux narines.***

(Wit Revived: How should one stop three holes with one thing?—By putting one man's nose in another man's - - - -.)

One type of saucy riddle is absent from the *Demandes joyeuses* as well as from Wynkyn's book; suprisingly, for it had been enjoyed for centuries. This is the riddle, often in verse, that makes ladies blush and giggle because it lures them into thinking of an erotic answer—only to be abashed with an innocent one. Among the manuscripts of Exeter Cathedral there is a collection known as the Exeter Book containing verse riddles in Old English dating probably from the eighth century. Scholars agree that in a number of cases where such answers as poker, knife-and-sheath, bagpipe, and dough (rising; thrust by a woman into her oven) are possible, an erotic meaning suggests itself first. Such things were not seldom the amusement of medieval churchmen. In Czechoslovakia there survives a collection of 136 riddles that were put into Latin hexameters about the year 1365 by a Benedictine monk known as Claretus or Claret. About a quarter of them have open or covert obscene meanings. Here is an example in a modern translation:

A vessel I have/That is round like a pear/
Moist in the middle/Surrounded with hair/
And often it happens/That water flows there.

(Solution: Eye)

It is not unfitting that verse is used in many languages for this sort of double-meaning play, for it is near to the metaphor of poetry. It enriches the songs, especially the love-songs, of all ages. In a manuscript of the first half of the fifteenth century (Sloane 2593 in the British Museum), there is a charming lyric that begins:

I have a new garden
And new is begun.
Such another garden
Know I not under sun.
In the midst of my garden
Is a perier [pear-tree] set
And it will none pear bearen
But a pear jennet.
The fairest maid of this town
Prayed me
For to graft her a graft
Of mine perry tree . . .

And a graft she got, 'And by that day twenty weeks/It was quick in her womb . . .' There can hardly be any doubt that the 'I had a little nut-tree' song (which might sing to the same tune) is saying the same thing; which accounts for the King of Spain's daughter travelling so far.

The same fifteenth-century manuscript has another song that is presented directly as a riddle:

I have a pocket for the nonce.
Therein be twain precious stones.
Damsel, had ye essayed them once
  Ye should the rather go with me.
I have a (illegible) of God's sonde [making].
Withouten feet it can stand.
It can smite and has none hand:
  Rid [riddle] yourself what it may be.

One might say this is more honest because it does not offer a second meaning. The two kinds went on being enjoyed side by side. There are some of the double-meaning type in another French riddle book, ***Les Adevineaux Amoureux*** (The Amorous Riddles), printed at Bruges long before 1500. This book is interesting because among ten riddles it has in common with Wynkyn de Worde's book, three (Nos. 12, 45 and 47) are not in *Demandes joyeuses*. An example of a double-meaning verse in *Les Adevineaux* is:

Entre deux jambes le vif amble,
Entre deux fesses le vif tremble,
Et quand il vient a la porte,
Son maître busque.
—C'est un chevalier monté sur une haghenée.
(Between two legs the living flesh ambles,
Between two buttocks the living flesh trembles,
And when it comes to the door,
Its master knocks.
—This is a rider mounted on a hackney.)

In the sixteenth century several Italians devoted a great deal of poetic ingenuity to this type of riddle. The best known is Giovanfrancesco Straparola, whose Boccaccian tales of 1550-53, *Piacevoli Notti,* are accompanied by seventy-four riddles, among which the suggestive qualities of a bagpipe, mortar and pestle, glove, lock, lute, pen, syringe, trumpet, warming-pan, candle and many other things are made use of. Straparola and another practitioner, Tommaso Stigliani, were put on the Vatican's Index of banned books in 1604. Six years before that, a few riddles from Straparola and a few from a Frenchman, Pierre de Larivey, appeared in translation in a book with an unjustified title, *The Riddles of Heraclitus and Democritus.* Here is its version of Straparola's candle:

All day like one that's in disgrace
He resteth in some secret place,
And seldom putteth forth the head
Until daylight be fully fled.
Then in the maid's or goodwife's hand

The gallant 'gins first up to stand:
Whom to a hole they do apply
Wherein he will both live and die.

This book was aimed at gentlemen, as its title shows. In books for the popular market, at this time and later, double meanings were extremely rare. Gentlemen's private manuscripts, however, were another matter. They often contain a good deal of bawdy material, passed on from generation to generation. The candle verses and four other items from ***The Riddles of Heraclitus*** appear in a collection made by the Randle Holme family of Chester (MS. Harl.1960 in the British Museum) in the second and third quarters of the seventeenth century. This collection incidentally demonstrates the vitality of certain riddles, for it contains Nos. 12, 45, 46 and 47 of ***Demaundes Joyous.*** Of its 140-odd items, about one-sixth have obscene double meanings. It has two versions of a 'gooseberry' riddle that is found time and again in seventeenth century gentlemen's manuscripts (but only once in print, in ***Wit and Drollery,*** 1656, one of the bawdy Cavalier collections put out in Cromwell's time). This riddle has echoes of the early fifteenth-century manuscript I have quoted:

There is a bush fit for the nonce
That beareth pricks and precious stones
The fruit in fear some ladies pull.
Tis smooth and round and plump and full...
They put it in, and then they move it,
Which makes it melt, and then they love it.
So what was round, plump, full and hard
Grows lank and thin and dull and marred...

The fifteenth-century manuscript is echoed, too, in another riddle-verse found in many seventeenth century manuscripts:

> It is a kind of pleasing thing,
> A pricking and a piercing sting.
> It is Venus' wanton wand.
> It hath no legs and yet can stand . . .

The suggestive riddle was occasionally used by the singers of merry catches. One by John Eccles (1668-1735), who was Master of the King's Band of Music, begins:

> My man John had a thing that was long.
> My maid Mary had a thing that was hairy.
> My man John put his thing that was long
> Into my maid Mary's thing that was hairy.

The songbook (I quote *The Catch Club or Merry Companions,* 1733) explains the riddle: 'Maid Mary having broke the handle of her hair broom, and hearing that Man John had a long stick that would fit it, desir'd him to put it in for her.' The broom demands a good deal of labour from John—

> Till wearied and vexed and with knocking grown sore,
> Cried, 'A pox take the hole, for I'll knock it no more.'

But these *jeux d'esprit* are taking this study too far beyond 1511. It is time to look at two English riddle books that are in a direct line of inheritance from *The Demaundes Joyous.*

The earlier one, unluckily, survives only in two fragments, of about four inches by six, that were rescued from the binding of an old book. One fragment is now in the Bodleian Library and the other in the Edinburgh University Library. They were printed about twenty years after Wynkyn's book, and are ascribed to William Rastell (whose father printed the *Hundred*

Merry Tales mentioned earlier). Perhaps this near-phantom of a riddle book was called the *Hundred Merry Riddles;* certainly it contained one hundred, for one fragment bears the words, '[Heareaf]ter foloweth the solucyons of the C rydyllys,' followed by the solutions to the first three and part of the fourth. The fragments also provide, though with some missing words, ten riddles from three separate parts of the book, so that directly or indirectly we have fourteen of the hundred. Three of these fourteen are from **Wynkyn's book** (our Nos. 24, 43 and 51), a proportion that suggests that twenty-one of the hundred may have been from this source. No. 24 is reworded: 'To what poor man is a man's alms worst bestowed?' No. 43 drops the phrase 'in no wise': 'What folk be they that love not to be prayed for?' No. 51 is exactly as in the original: 'What man is he that getteth his living backward?'

The next thing that the fragments show is that in the Hundred Riddles, double-meaning folk riddles were, for once, put into print. They stood boldly at the beginning of the book, too, as we may see by the surviving 'solucyons' to the first four items. A few words have been cut away, but they are easily deduced in the context. The solution to No. 1 read: 'It is a furred glove. But this riddle must be put by a woman, or else it is not proper.' That warning is a genial sop to possible objectors, and comes rather late. The riddle will have said something to the effect of, 'I push my naked thing into the warm fur-fringed thing.' This occurs in many collections of folk riddles; sometimes there are variants in which feet are thrust into hairy stockings, or (in the Exeter Riddles) heads into shirts. The solution to No. 2 read: 'It is a distaff; for the distaff standeth and the flax hangeth.' The riddle will have played on the distaff's being held between a woman's legs: just as Sir Toby Belch does (*Twelfth Night*, I, iii) when he compares Aguecheek to a distaff and says, 'I hope to see a housewife take thee between her legs and spin it off.' Solution No. 3: 'It is a wafer, which goeth into a cup of wine stiff standing, and cometh out lithe and dropping.' Variations of this, too, are frequent in folk collections. The Holme riddles of the next century have a variant with a carrot boiled in a pot. In recent times in America, riddle collectors have found this:

When it goes in it's stiff and stout.
When it comes out it's flopping about. (Cabbage)

Solution No. 4 (half missing): 'It is a pair of bellows; for there is the hole that receiveth the air, which is the gap; and thereon is a leather flap; and . . . .'
I hesitate to reconstruct the riddle, but the possibilities can be guessed. The words 'gap' and 'flap' suggest that it was in rhyme.

The fragments show, finally, that Rastell's book of about 1530 contributed generously to a collection that remained popular until the eighteenth century, *The Booke of Merrie Riddles* (styled BMR hereafter). In fact, BMR seems to have been largely an expurgated version of the Hundred Riddles for a later, wider audience. Books hawked round the country by the competitive publishers of Shakespeare's time and later had to be acceptable to modest housewives. There is not one naughty double meaning in BMR, and it avoids such dubious things as cleanliest leaves and farting maidens. At what date the cleaning-up took place it is impossible to say, but it was probably in Queen Elizabeth's time. An edition of 1600 was recorded in the nineteenth century. The earliest now known is dated 1617; it's page-by-page headline is 'The Booke of Riddles', and that was probably the earlier title. A 'Booke of Riddles' is mentioned in a list of 1575. (Of course, this may have been an edition of the 1530 book). In any case, large sections of the old book were certainly taken over in BMR, on the evidence of the fragments. Riddles No. 45-47 in the fragments are 26-28 in BMR; Nos. 55-57 are 35-37 in BMR; and Nos. 98-9 are 67-8. The picture that emerges is that nineteen questionable riddles were thrown out at the beginning and a further dozen at intervals. Then a few new ones were added at the end, for BMR has seventy-six in all. In the process, BMR retained twelve riddles from *Demaundes Joyous:* the three that are in the fragments, and Nos. 1, 4, 6, 11, 12, 37, 46, 47 and 53. The wording of many of them remains very near to that of *Demaundes Joyous.* For example, the BMR version of our No. 47 reads (even in the later seventeenth century), 'What was he that was begotten ere his father, born ere his mother, and had the maidenhead of his grandame?' But sometimes—as I show in my notes—BMR turns the prose Demaundes into verse, or feels a need to give laborious explanations.

A few of the other riddles that BMR took from the 1530 book are worth recording.

Ten men's length
And ten men's strength
And ten men cannot set it on end. (A Rope)

What is that that goeth through the wood and
toucheth never a twist [in BMR, *a twig*]?
—It is the blast of a horn.

What is it—
That hath five legs on the one side, and three on
the other,
Heads three, and ears six, and two things like my
mother,

And yet such another thing as hath my brother?
—It is a man and a woman upon a mare's back.
[The woman sits sideways.]

What three heads be they that uphold the world?
—Those be the hammer-head, the plough-head,
and the head that multiplieth the world.

Here, in a variation of No. 48 in *Demaundes Joyous*, is one faint surviving hint of indecorousness in BMR; and perhaps the preceding riddle is another.

By the second half of Elizabeth's reign, all this was coming to be regarded as rather beneath anyone who aspired to be thought a courtly wit. In *The English Courtier* of 1586, a dialogue on court and country life in which the court tends to be favoured, it is the country gentleman who mentions the *Hundred Merry Tales* and the *Book of Riddles* among his 'witty and pleasant' books. 'These pretty and pithy matters,' he says, 'do sometimes recreate our minds, chiefly after long sitting and loss of money [at gaming].' About ten years later, it is that simple (too simple) country gentleman, Slender, who wishes, in the first scene of *The Merry Wives of Windsor*, that he had his *Book of Riddles* with him to give him something clever to say to Anne Page. But in the time of Henry VIII, riddles were welcome at court. The Shakespearian actor Robert Armin, writing in 1600, tells in his book *Foole upon Foole* how Henry VIII's jester Will Sommers undertook to get the king out of a mood of 'extreme melancholy' by asking him three riddles. 'That Will Sommers asked them of the king, it is certain,' he says. 'There are some will affirm it now living at Greenwich [the royal palace, where Sommers lived on until 1560].' The first riddle is our No. 37. The second is our No. 34—but as Armin retells it, it is less coarse and less pointed:

'Marry,' says Will, 'I say a dirt-dauber.'
'Out on it!' says the king. 'That is the foulest, for he is dirty up to the elbows.'
'Aye,' says Will, 'but then he washes them clean again, and eats his meat cleanly enough.'

The third riddle goes like this:

'Now tell me,' says Will, 'if you can, what it is, that being born without life, head, lip or eye, yet doth run roaring through the world till it die?'
'This is a wonder,' quod the king, 'and no question. I know it not.'
'Why,' quod Will, 'it is a fart.'
At this the king laughed heartily and was exceeding merry....

This one was no invention of Will's. It was international. In *Les Adevineaux Amoureux* it goes like this:

Adevinez que c'est:
Quand il nait il brait,
Et quand il est nait
Il se tait.
—C'est le haut vent issant du trou sur quoi on sied.
(Guess what this is: As it is born it cries out, and when it is born it becomes silent.
—It is the high wind issuing from the hole on which one sits.)

The words that Will Sommers actually spoke to Henry VIII were very likely in verse too:

What is born without life, head, lip or eye,
Yet runs roaring through the world till it die?

Perhaps Will found all three riddles in the Hundred Riddles book, which came out at just the right time for him; perhaps he had an old copy of *The Demaundes Joyous* too. All merry books would be useful to a jester in a time when great men were glad to laugh at such wise, purging, simple things.

Our jesters now have, it may be, subtler scripts to ease our melancholy. But the old riddle books still delight us with their pithy and pretty matters, and they bring us nearer to the men who bought these books by thousands and read them almost into oblivion.

¶ The demaũdes Joyous.

Demaunde. Who bare yͤ beſt burden that
euer was borne. ℞. That bare yͤ aſſe whã
our lady fled with our lorde in to egypte.
¶Demaunde. Where became yͤ aſſe that
our lady rode vpon. ℞. Adams moder de
de ete her. ¶Demaunde. Who was Adams moder.
℞. The erthe. ¶Demaunde. What ſpace is from yͤ hy
eſt ſpace of the ſe to the depeſt. ℞. But a ſtones caſt
¶Demaũde. Whã antecryſt is come in to this worl-
de what thynge ſhall be hardeſt to hym to knowe. ℞.
A hande barowe / for of that he ſhall not knowe whi-
che ende ſhall goo before. ¶Demaunde. How many
calues tayles behoueth to reche frome the erthe to the
ſkye. ℞. No more but one & it be longe ynough. ¶De
maunde How many holy dayes be there ĩ the yere yͭ
neuer fall on the ſondayes. ℞. There be eyght that is
to wete yͤ thre holy dayes after Eeſter. iii. after whyt-
ſondaye / the holy aſcencyon daye / and corpus cryſty
daye. ¶Demaũde. Whiche ben yͤ trulyeſt tolde thyn-
ges in the worlde. ℞. Thoſe be yͤ ſteyres of chambres
and houſes. ¶Demaunde. Whiche parte of a ſergeaũ
te loue ye beſt towarde you. ℞. His heles. ¶Demaũ-
de. Whiche is the beſt wood and leeſt brente. ℞. Vy-
nes. ¶Demaunde. Whiche is the mooſt profytable
beeſt & that men eteth leeſt of. ℞. That is bees. ¶De
maunde. Whiche is the brodeſt water and leeſt Jeo-
perdye to paſſe ouer. ℞. The dewe. ¶Demaunde.
What thynges is it that the more that one drynketh yͤ
leſſe he ſhall pyſſe. ℞. It is fartes & fyeſtes / for who
that drynketh a hondreth thouſande they ſhall neuer

pysse a droppe. ¶ Demaunde what thynge is it that
neuer was nor neuer shall be. R. Neuer mouse ma=
de her nest in a cattes ere. ¶ Demaunde. Why dryue
men dogges out of the chyrche. R. Bycause they co=
me not vp and offre. ¶ Demaunde. Why come dog=
ges so often to the chyrche. R. Bycause whan they se
the aulters couered they wene theyr maysters goo
thyder to dyner. ¶ Demaunde. Why dooth a dogge
tourne hym thryes a boute or ye he lyeth hym downe.
R. Bycause he knoweth not his beddes hede frome
the fete. ¶ Demaunde. Why doo men make an ouen
in the towne. R. For bycause they can not make the
towne in the ouen. ¶ Demaunde. What beest is it
that hath her tayle bytwene her eyen. R. it is a catte
whan she lycketh her arse. ¶ Demaunde. Whiche is
the moost cleynlyest lefe amonge all other leues. R. it
is holly leues / for noo body wyll not wype his arse
with them. ¶ Demaunde. Who was he that lete the
fyrst farte at rome. R. That was the arse. ¶ Demaū=
de. How may a man knowe or perceyue a cowe in a
flocke of shepe. R. By syghte. ¶ Demaunde. What
thynge is it that hathe hornes at the arse. R. It is a
sacke. ¶ Demaunde. What almes is worst bestowed
that men gyue. R. That is to a blynde man / for as
he hathe ony thynge gyuen hym / he wolde with good
wyll se hym hanged by the necke that gaue it hym.
¶ Demaunde. Wherfore set they vpon chyrche ste=
ples more a cocke than a henne. R. yf men sholde sette
there a henne seh wolde laye egges / and tehy wolde
fall vpon mennes hedes. ¶ Demaunde what thynge
is it that hathe none ende. R. A bowle. ¶ Demaun=

de. What wode is it that neuer flyes reste vpon. R. The claper of a lazers dysshe. Demaũde how wolde ye saye two pater nosters for your frendes soule / and god neuer made but one pater noster. R. Saye one two tymes. Demaunde whiche ben the moost profytable sayntes in the chyrche. R. They that stonde in ÿ glasse wyndowes / for they kepe out ÿ wynde for wastynge of the lyght. Demaũde. What people be they ÿ neuer go a processyon. R. They be those that rynge ÿ belles ein ÿ meane season. Demaũde what is it ÿ freseth neuer. R. That is hote water. Demaũde. What thӯge is that / ÿ is moost lykest vnto a hors. R. That is a mare. ¶ Demaũde. Wherfore be there not as many women conteyned in ÿ daunce of poules as there be men. R. By cause a women is so ferefull of herte that she had leuer daunce amonge quycke folke than deed. ¶ Demaunde whiche is the clenlyest occupacyon that is. R. That is a dauber / for he may neyther shyte nor ete tyll he hath wasshed his handes. ¶ Demaunde. What daye in the yere ben the flyes moost aferde. R. That is on palme sonday whã they se euery body haue an handeful of palme in theyr hande / they wene it is to kyll theym wt. ¶ Demaunde what tyme of the yere may maydens moost with theyr honeste kyest in the chyrche. R. In lent season / for than euery sayntes nose and face is couered so that they smell no thynge. ¶ Demaunde. What thynge is it the lesse it is the more it is dredde. R. A brydge. ¶ Demaunde. Wherfore is it that yonge chyldren wepe as soone as euer they ben borne. R. Bycause theyr moder is noo more mayden. ¶ Demaunde. Wherfore is it that an asse hathe so grete eres. R. Bycause her moder put no begyn on her heed in her yought. ¶ Demaūde what is it that is a wryte and is no man / and he dothe that no man can / and yet it serueth bothe god and man. R. That is a be. ¶ Demaūde. Whiche was fyrst ẏ henne or ẏ egge. R. The henne whā god made her. ¶ Demaunde. Why dothe an oxe or a cowe lye. R. Bycause she can not sytte. ¶ Demaūde what people be they that loue not in no wyse to be prayed for. R. They be beggers & poore people whā men say god helpe them whan they aske almes. ¶ Demaūde. How many strawes go to a gose nest. R. None for lacke of fete. ¶ Demaunde. What tyme in the yere bereth a gose moost feders. R. Whan the gander is vpon her backe. ¶ Demaunde what was he that slewe the fourth parte of the worlde. R. Cayne whan that he slewe his broder abell in the whiche tyme was but foure persones in the worlde. ¶ Demaunde. What was he that was begoten or his fader / and borne or his moder / and had the maydenhede of his beldame. R. That was Abell. ¶ Demaunde. What thre thynges be they that the worlde is moost mayntened by. R. That is to wete by wordes erbes and stones. Why with wordes man worshyppeth god / and as of erbes that is all maner of corne that man is fedde with / and as stones one is that gryndeth the corne and the other encreaseth the worlde. De. What is ẏ aege of a felde mous. R. A yere And a hedge may stande thre mous lyues / and the lyfe of a dogge is the terme of thre hedges standynge & the lyfe of a hors is thre dogges lyues / and the lyfe of a man is thre hors lyues / and the lyfe of a gose is thre

mennes lyues /and yͤ lyfe of a ſwanne thre goſe lyues
and the lyfe of a ſwalowe is thre ſwanne lyues and
the lyfe of an egle is thre ſwalowes lyues/and the ly=
fe of a ſerpent is thre egles lyues/and the lyfe of a ra=
uen is thre ſerpentes lyues /and the lyfe of a harte is
thre rauens lyues / and an oke groweth. v. hondreth
yere / and it ſtandeth in one ſtate fyue hondreth yere
and it fadeth fyue hondreth yere beſyde the rote why
che doubleth thre tymes euerych of the thre aeges a
foreſayd. ¶Demaunde. A man had thre doughters
of thre aeges /whiche doughters he delyuered to ſell
certayne apples/and he toke to the ledeſt doughter. l.
apples/and to the ſeconde. xxx. apples/and to the yon
geſt ten apples /and all theſe thre ſolde in lyke many
for a peny / and brought home in lyke moche money
now how many ſolde eche of them for a peny. R. The
yongeſt ſolde fyrſt ſeuen for a peny/and the other two
ſyſters ſolde after the ſame pryce / than yͤ eldeſt ſyſter
had one odde apple lefte /and the ſeconde ſyſter two /
and the yongeſt thre apples / now theſe apples lyked
the byer ſoo well that in contynent he came agayne to
the yongeſt ſyſter and bought of her thre apples after
thre pens a pece/than had ſhe ten pens/and the ſecon
de thoughte ſhe wolde kepe the ſame pryce/and ſolde
her two apples for thre pens a pece and than had ſhe
ten pens /& yͤ eldeſt ſolde her one apple for thre pens/
& than had ſhe ten pens/thus ſolde they in lyke many
apples for a peny and broughte home in lyke moche
money. ¶Demaunde. What man is he that geteth his
lyuynge bacwarde. reſ. That is rope maker. ¶De=
maunde. What people be tho that geteth theyr lyuyn=

ge moost merylyest. R. Tho be prestes & fullers / for one syngeth and the other daunceth. ¶ Demaunde. What is he that made all and solde all / & he yͤ bought all loste all. R. A smyth made an alle and solde it / and the shomaker yͤ bought it lost it. ¶ Demaunde whether is it bett to lyue by thefte or by almes dedes. R. The rewarde of thefte is to be hanged / and yf thou lyue by almes dedes that is by beggers tordes.

¶ Thus endeth yͤ Demaundes Joyous
Enprynted at London iu Flete stre
te at the sygne of the sonne by
me Wynkyn de Worde.
In the yere of our
lorde a M.
CCCCC.
and xi.

W C
d
wynkyn
worde.

(dj) after a number indicates that the riddle is from the French *Demandes joyeuses.*
BMR=*The Booke of Merrie Riddles.*

1 (dj) Who bare the best burden that ever was borne?
That bare the ass when Our Lady fled with Our Lord into Egypt.

2 Where became the ass that Our Lady rode upon?
Adam's mother did eat her.

3 Who was Adam's mother?
The earth.

4 (dj) What space is from the highest space of the sea to the deepest?
But a stone's cast.
BMR helpfully adds, '. . . for a stone thrown in, be it never so deep, will go the the bottom.'

5 (dj) When Antichrist is come into this world, what thing shall be hardest to him to know?
A hand-barrow; for of that he shall not know which end shall go before.
'Hand-barrow' here is not a wheelbarrow, but a wheel-less thing like a stretcher, with handles at both ends.

6 (dj) How many calves' tails behoveth to reach from the earth to the sky?
No more but one, and [if] ***it be long enough.***
Folk versions of this also use pigs' tails, hairs, and ladders.

7 How many holy days be there in the year, that never fall on the Sundays?
There be eight; that is, to wit, the three holy

days after Easter, three after Whitsunday, the holy Ascension Day, and Corpus Christi day.

8 Which be the truliest told things in the world?
Those be the stairs of chambers and houses.

9 Which part of a sergeant love ye best toward you?
His heels.
sergeant: a police officer.

10 Which is the best wood and least burnt?
Vines.

11 Which is the most profitable beast and that men eateth least of?
That is bees.
BMR explains: 'It is a bee, for it maketh both honey and wax, and yet costeth his master nothing the keeping.'

12 Which is the broadest water and least jeopardy to pass over?
The dew.
BMR versifies this:

A water there is which I must pass,
A broader water there never was,
And yet of all waters I ever see
To pass it over is least jeopardy.

13 (dj) What things is it, that the more that one drinketh the less he shall piss?
It is farts and fyestes [fizzles], ***for who that drinketh a hundred thousand, they shall never piss a drop.***
drinketh: This was long a usage for things breathed in; in the seventeenth century, for smoking a pipe.

14 (dj) What thing is it that never was nor never shall be?
Never mouse made her nest in a cat's ear.

15 (dj) Why drive men dogs out of the church?
Because they come not up and offer.
An additional reason in the French is censored in the English: '*Et aussi parce qu'ils chient sur les morts.*' (And also because they shit on the dead.)

16 (dj) Why come dogs so often to the church?
Because when they see the altars covered, they ween [think] ***their masters go thither to dinner.***

17 (dj) Why doth a dog turn him thrice about ere he lieth him down?
Because he knoweth not his bed's head from the feet.

18 (dj) Why do men make an oven in the town?
For because they cannot make the town in the oven.

19 (dj) What beast is it that hath her tail between her eyes?
It is a cat when she licketh her arse.
A slight variant in the earlier *Adevineaux Amoureux* reads: '*Qui est la bête qui a sa tête entre ses jambes?—C'est un chat qui lèche son cul, sauve honneur*. (The last two words are an apology for a rudery; like the 'saving your reverence' of sixteenth-century England.)

In a manuscript of James I's time (Add. 5956 in British Museum), which was apparently used for barristers' entertainments, there is a cousin of the cat riddle: 'When is a cow roundest?—When she licketh her arse.' This manuscript also has our Nos. 17 and 45, as well as a coarse dog riddle: 'Why doth a dog hold up his leg to piss?—Because he hath never a hand to pull out his prick.'

20 Which is the most cleanliest leaf among all other leaves?

It is holly leaves; for nobody will not wipe his arse with them.

21 (dj) Who was he that let the first fart at Rome?
That was the [Pope's] ***arse.***
The correct answer is given in *Demandes joyeuses:* '*Le cul du pape.*' Whether Wynkyn de Worde left the pope out by accident or through prudence is an interesting speculation.

22 (dj) How may a man know or perceive a cow in a flock of sheep?
By sight.

23 (dj) What thing is it that hath horns at the arse?
It is a sack.

24 (dj) What alms is worst bestowed that men give?
That is to a blind man; for as he hath anything given him, he would with good will see him hanged by the neck that gave it him.
The vital word, of course, is 'see'.

25 (dj) Wherefore set they upon church steeples more a cock than a hen?
If men should set there a hen, she would lay eggs, and they would fall upon men's heads.
The English version is a nice improvement on the French, which reads: *Parce que si la géline* [*hen*] *pondait, les oeufs se casseraient* [the eggs would break].

26 What thing is it that hath none end?
A bowl.

27 What wood is it that never flies rest upon?
The clapper of a lazar's dish.
lazar's dish: beggar's bowl.

28 (dj) How would ye say two paternosters for your friend's soul, and God never made but one paternoster?
Say one two times.

This is a reworking of the French version: *Comment diriez-vous deux paternostres pour un votre ami? On n'en pourrait-pas dire deux, car dieu n'en fait jamais qu'une.* (How would you say two . . .? You could not say two, for God never made but one.)

29 **Which be the most profitable saints in the church?**

They that stand in the glass windows, for they keep out the wind for wasting of the light.

30 (dj) **What people be they that never go a procession?**

They be those that ring the bells in the mean season.

31 **What is it that freezeth never?**

That is hot water.

32 (dj) **What thing is that that is most likest unto a horse?**

That is a mare.

The English version substitutes horses for the cats of the French original, which would lose their point on translation: *Qu'est-ce que mieux ressemble a un chat en une fenêtre?—C'est une chatte.* But the cats return in a London collection of 1655, *Wit Revived:* What is the likest to a cat in a hole? A cat out of a hole.

33 **Wherefore be there not as many women contained in the Dance of Paul's as there be men?**

Because a woman is so fearful of heart that she had liever dance among quick folk than dead.

The Dance of Paul's was a fifteenth-century Dance of Death mural, 'curiously painted upon board, about the north cloister of Paul's,' says John Stow in his Survey of London. It was a copy of one in Paris, and showed 'Death leading all estates [ranks of men], with the speeches of Death, and answer of every estate.' The words, in verse, 'were translated out of French into English by John Lydgate . . . in the reign of Henry VI.' This cloister was pulled down in 1549, when the Protestant Edward VI was on the throne.

The riddle is of the zany type, like 15 and 16.

34 Which is the cleanliest occupation that is?
That is a dauber; for he may neither shite nor eat till he hath washed his hands.

dauber: a man who applied the daub or plaster to houses. This riddle is not in French collections; but it is in a collection of stories ascribed to the jovial Florentine priest and merchant Arlotto Mainardi (1395–1484). He and his friends sit discussing who is the cleanest craftsman. He dismisses their reasonable suggestions: the cleanest are *li fornacai* (workers in brick-and-tile kilns) *perchè non vanno mai a cacare che non si lavino prima le mani* (because they never go to shit without first washing their hands). Arlotto was in the wool trade, travelled to England, and is on record as having amused Edward IV. Perhaps he brought the joke to England; or found it here and took it to Italy.

35 What day in the year be the flies most a-feared?
That is on Palm Sunday, when they see everybody have a handful of palm in their hand; they ween it is to kill them with.

36 (dj) What time of the year may maidens most with their honesty fyest [fizzle] in the church?
In Lent season; for then every saint's nose and face is covered so that they smell nothing.

37 (dj) **What thing is it, the less it is the more it is dread?**
A bridge.
BMR gives a twenty-nine-word explanation of this.

38 (dj) **Wherefore is it that young children weep as soon as ever they be born?**
Because their mother is no more maiden.
In the French there is an additional reason: '. . . *et qu'ils ont baisé leur cul* (and because they have kissed their—the mothers'—arses).

39 (dj) **Wherefore is it that an ass hath so great ears?**
Because her mother put no biggin on her head in her youth.
biggin: a baby's close-fitting hood.

Perhaps Rabelais found this riddle in *Demandes joyeuses.* In Book II, chapter 16 of his great work, he has Panurge say, 'That which makes asses to have such great ears is, that their dams did put no biggins on their heads.' Panurge cites this in support of his explanation why 'friars had so long and large genitories,' which is 'that they wear no bottomed breeches . . .'

40 **What is it that is a wright and is no man, and he doth that** [that which] **no man can, and yet it serveth both God and man?**
That is a bee.

41 Which was first, the hen or the egg?
The hen, when God made her.

42 (dj) **Why doth an ox or a cow lie?**
Because she cannot sit.
Silly questions have been getting silly answers for a long time. Bar-Hebraeus, head of the Christian church in Syria from 1264 to 1286, made a collection of stories and jokes in which we find this: 'When

a cock wakes in the morning, why does he hold one foot in the air?—If he lifted both he would fall down.'

An old Irish riddle translates like this: 'Why does the duck stand on one leg?—To give a rest to the other leg.'

43 (dj) What people be they that love not in no wise to be prayed for?
They be beggars and poor people, when men say 'God help them' when they ask alms.

44 How many straws go to a goose nest?
None, for lack of feet.

45 (dj) What time in the year beareth a goose most feathers?
When the gander is upon her back.

The English version is a less erotic alternative for the French, which reads: *En quel temps est une femme plus douce?—Quand elle laisse l'homme monter sur elle.* The seventeenth-century Holme manuscript (Harl. 1960) introduces another creature: 'What time in the year is it that a cow hath most flesh and a goose most feathers . . . ?'

46 What was he that slew the fourth part of the world?
Cain when he slew his brother Abel, in the which time was but four persons in the world.

47 What was he that was begotten ere his father, and born ere his mother, and had the maidenhead of his beldame?
That was Abel.

These two riddles and variations of them were evidently current throughout medieval Europe. In the early fourteenth-century verse collection in Middle English, the *Cursor Mundi*, a poem beginning

'Quen Adam Abels bodi fand' has the lines (with slight modernisation):

This is that man, men say, was born
Both his father and mother beforn.
He had his eldemother's maidenhead,
And at his burying all manner leid [grief].

The Anglo-Saxon *Dialogue of Salomon and Saturnus,* which dates perhaps from the ninth century, has this among its questions and answers: 'Who was he that was never born, was then buried in his mother's womb, and after death was baptised?—That was Adam.' Among the fourteenth-century riddles of the Bohemian monk Claretus is one saying the same thing: '*Non natus moritur, utero matris sepelitur . . .*'

The late fifteenth-century *Adevineaux Amoureux* puts the Abel riddle into verse: '*Je fus né devant devant mon père/Et engendrez devant ma mère, etc.*' As late as 1792, in *A Choice Collection of Riddles, Charades, Rebusses,* Eve appears:

In a garden was laid
A most beautiful maid
As ever was seen in the morn;
She was made a wife
The first day of her life,
And died before she was born.

48 What three things be they that the world is most maintained by?

That is, to wit, by words, herbs and stones. Why: with words man worshippeth God; and as of herbs, that is all manner of corn that man is fed with; and as stones, one is that grindeth the corn, and the other increaseth the world.

The 'stones' that increase the world—that is,

increase the men and animals in it—are testicles.

49 What is the age of a fieldmouse?
A year. And a hedge may stand three mouse lives, and the life of a dog is the term of three hedges' standing, and the life of a horse is three dogs' lives, and the life of a man is three horse lives, and the life of a goose is three men's lives, and the life of a swan three goose lives, and the life of a swallow is three swan lives, and the life of an eagle is three swallows' lives, and the life of a serpent is three eagles' lives, and the life of a raven is three serpents' lives, and the life of a hart is three ravens' lives, and an oak groweth five hundred year, and it standeth in one state five hundred year, and it fadeth five hundred year, besides the rot, which doubleth three times every one of the three ages aforesaid.
This piece of folk science grows progressively more nonsensical after 'the life of a man is three horse lives'.

50 A man had three daughters of three ages; which daughters he delivered, to sell, certain apples. And he took to the eldest daughter fifty apples, and to the second thirty apples, and to the youngest ten apples; and all these three sold in like many [the same number] for a penny, and brought home in like much money [the same sum of money]. Now how many sold each of them for a penny?
The youngest sold first seven for a penny, and the other two sisters sold after the same price. Then the eldest sister had one odd apple left, and the second sister two, and the youngest

three apples. Now these apples liked the buyer so well that incontinent [straight away] ***he came again to the youngest sister and bought of her three apples after threepence apiece; then had she tenpence. And the second thought she would keep the same price, and sold her two apples for threepence apiece; and then had she tenpence. And the eldest sold her one apple for threepence; and then had she tenpence. Thus sold they in like many apples for a penny and brought home in like much money.***

The point is that the eldest daughter sold forty-nine apples at seven for a penny, and the second twenty-eight at seven for a penny.

51 (dj) What man is he that getteth his living backward?

That is a ropemaker.

The BMR explanation is for once useful to modern readers: '. . . for as he maketh his ropes he goeth backward'.

52 (dj) What people be they that getteth their living most merriliest?

They be priests and fullers; for one singeth and the other danceth.

In processing new-woven cloth, fullers would tread up and down on it in vats.

53 What is he that made all and sold all, and he that bought all lost all?

A smith made an awl and sold it, and the shoemaker that bought it lost it.

54 Whether is it better to live by theft or by alms deeds?

The reward of theft is to be hanged; and if

thou live by alms deeds, that is by beggars' turds.

In old slang, turds left by beggars at the roadside were called alms deeds because they were the beggars' only gifts to their fellow-men. Another slang term was 'pilgrims' salve'.

Thus endeth the Demaundes Joyous
printed at London in Fleet
Street at the sign of the
Sun by me Wynkyn de Worde
in the year of Our Lord
MCCCCCXI

Wynkyn de Worde, a native of Wörth in the Duchy of Lorraine, was brought to England in about 1476 by William Caxton, with whom he worked at Westminster until the latter's death in 1491. Wynkyn de Worde inherited Caxton's business and continued printing at the sign of the Red Pale until he moved to Fleet Street, opposite the end of Shoe Lane, at the Sign of the Sun, in 1501. He printed books there until his death in the winter of 1534-35. He is buried in St. Bride's Church, London.

BIBLIOGRAPHY

Verbatim reprints of ***The Demaundes Joyous*** are very scarce. None appears to have been published for a hundred years. Even the British Museum library has only three:

1829, as an insertion in C. H. Hartshorne's ***Ancient Metrical Tales***, a collection of late medieval English verse from Cambridge manuscripts.

1841, in Thomas Wright and J. O. Halliwell's ***Reliquiae Antiquae***, a collection of medieval and early Renaissance English prose and verse.

1848, in J. M. Kemble's ***The Dialogue of Salomon and Saturnus*** (useful for the whole subject of the medieval question-and-answer form).

Cambridge University Library has in addition a copy of a facsimile edition of 100 copies (no date, no imprint), issued by E. W. Ashbee about 1870.

Collections of riddles and learned studies of them are listed copiously in the works of Archer Taylor cited below. A few other useful studies are given, together with the riddle sources named in the introduction.

Les Adevineaux Amoureux, Bruges, 1472. Reprinted Paris 1831, in old French popular literature series, ***Les Joyeusetez, Facécies et Folastre Imaginacions***. (The printer at Bruges was Mansion, with whom William Caxton worked before bringing the art of printing to England in 1476; and perhaps it was there that Caxton found his young assistant, Wynkyn de Worde.)

The Booke of Merrie Riddles – early editions: 1617, Folger Shakespeare Library, Washington, D.C.

1629, Bodleian, Oxford; Boston Public Library, Mass.; Huntington Library, San Marino, Calif.
1631, Bodleian.
1660, British Museum.
1672, Huntington Library.
1685, Pepysian Library, Cambridge.
(See also Halliwell)

The Catch Club, or Merry Companions, 1733.

Demandes joyeuses en maniere de quolibets. No date or place of publication in British Museum copy. French bibliographies list an edition printed about 1500 at Rouen.

de Filippis, Michelle, *The Literary Riddle in Italy at the End of the Sixteenth Century*, University of California Publications in Modern Philology, Vol 34, 1948 (especially for double-meaning riddles in verse).

Halliwell, J. O. (later Halliwell-Phillips), reprint of the 1629 *Booke of Merry Riddles* in *The Literature of the Sixteenth and Seventeenth Centuries Illustrated by Reprints of Very Rare Tracts*, 1851 (75 copies only).

——————— *The Booke of Merry Riddles*, 1866, reprint of 1660 edition (Halliwell destroyed all but ten copies).

Hull, Vernam, and Taylor, Archer, *A Collection of Irish Riddles*, University of California Press, Folklore Studies 6, 1955. Hundreds of riddles translated from the Irish and categorised.

Moran, James. *Wynkyn de Worde, Father of Fleet Street*, Wynkyn de Worde Society, London, 1963.

Peachy, Frederic, *Clareti Enigmata/The Latin Riddles of Claret*, University of California Press, Folklore Studies 7, 1957.

The Riddles of Heraclitus and Democritus, 1598.

Taylor, Archer, *A Bibliography of Riddles,* FF Communications No. 126, Helsinki, 1939.

— — — — — *English Riddles from Oral Tradition,* University of California Press, 1951(1,749 entries, exhaustively classified).

Tupper, Frederick, *The Holme Riddles* (*Ms. Harl.* 1960) Publications of the Modern Language Association of America, Vol. 18, 1903 (transcription of the manuscript, but expurgated).

— — — — — — *The Riddles of the Exeter Book,* Boston, 1910.

Wit Revived, by Asdryasdust Tossoffacan, 1655 ('toss off a can' of ale, that is).